The Mormons (The American
Religious Experience)
Jean Kinney Williams
AR B.L.: 8.8
Points: 3.0

THE MORMONS

THE MORMONS

JEAN KINNEY WILLIAMS

American Religious Experience

Franklin Watts
A Division of Grolier Publishing
New York / London / Hong Kong / Sydney
Danbury, Connecticut

Interior design by Molly Heron
Photo credits ©: The Church of Jesus Christ of Latter-Day Saints: cover; Bettmann Archive: 6,
19, 27, 31, 41, 45, 48, 55, 61, 63, 71, 74, 77, 82; LDS Historic Department Archives: 9, 16, 18, 23,
25, 29, 36, 52, 59, 85, 87, 91, 96; North Wind Picture Archives: 21; UPI/ Bettmann: 8, 10, 98;
Utah State Historical Society: 60.

Library of Congress Cataloging-in-Publication Data

Williams, Jean Kinney.
The Mormons / by Jean Kinney Williams.

p   .cm. — (American religious experience)
Summary: Includes a history of the Mormon Church, its general doctrines, practices, social
structure, place in American society, changes in beliefs, and conflicts with American society.
ISBN 0–531—11276–4
1. Church of Jesus Christ of Latter-day Saints—Juvenile literature. 2. Mormon Church—
Juvenile literature.   [1. Church of Jesus Christ of Latter-Day Saints. 2. Mormon Church.]
I. Title. II. Series.
BX8635.2.W59   1996
289.3—dc20   96–33829
                                                                          CIP
                                                                          ac

CONTENTS

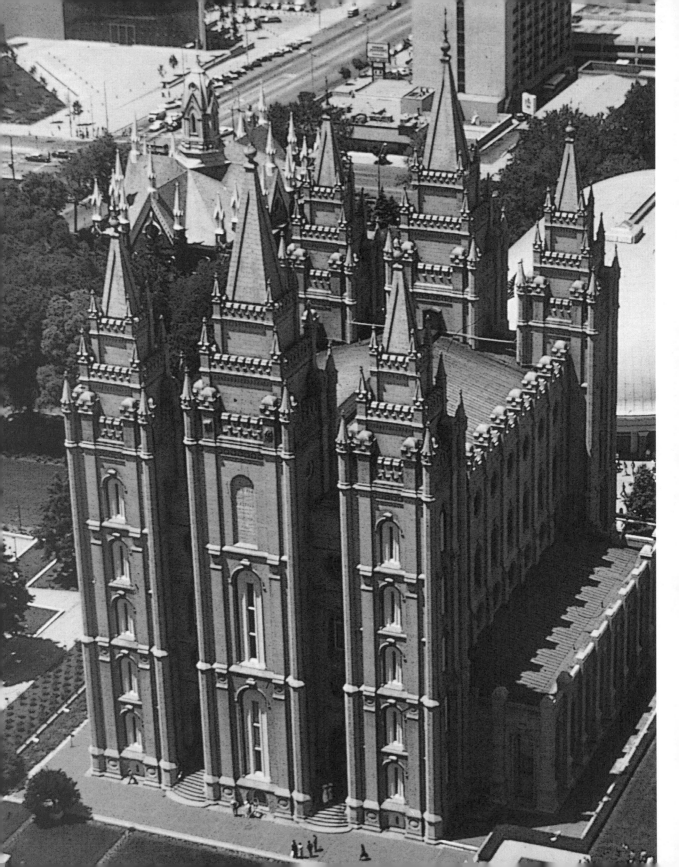

WHO ARE THE MORMONS?

1

The family gathered around the large table for dinner is like many others in modern America. The meal is simple to accommodate a big family on a careful budget. There is talk from the teenagers about band practice, science club meetings, and an after-school paper route, and everyone has various church meetings and obligations to discuss as well. Meanwhile, a baby, whose young married parents also are members of the household, is being passed from one set of eager arms to another.

The family of Lloyd and Judy Abbott feels very much at ease in their neighborhood, schools, and workplaces, an ease their ancestors were not so fortunate to experience. As members of the Church of Jesus Christ of Latter-day Saints, also known as the LDS or Mormon Church, Lloyd and Judy Abbott and their nine children are part of one of the fastest-growing churches in the United States and the world. The devotion of its members (4.5 million in the United States

The Mormon Tabernacle interior is a huge space. It houses a massive pipe organ and is home to the famous Mormon Tabernacle Choir.

and more than 9 million worldwide) and the highly organized structure of the church, with headquarters in Salt Lake City, Utah, have
helped it double in size between 1975 and 1995.

Perhaps the most famous image of the Latter-day Saints is that
of the Mormon Tabernacle Choir, which sings to packed halls all

over the globe. And it's not uncommon, traveling through neighborhoods in any American city, to see a pair of young, neatly dressed Mormon missionaries, calling on households to discuss their faith. Do you know anyone researching their family history? There's a good chance they'll be advised to seek out the vast genealogical records that the LDS church maintains in Salt Lake City.

But the acceptance that Latter-day Saints have won in the United States and around the world did not come easily. Judy and

The Whitmer family farmhouse was the site of the first meeting of the Mormon church.

Joseph Smith, founder of the Church of Jesus Christ of Latter-day Saints

Lloyd Abbott's ancestors, members of the church since its earliest days, moved from one settlement to another as the Latter-day Saints sought a place to live their religious convictions in peace. Those convictions won many converts, and the church has never stopped growing since it began with six members in a New York farmhouse in 1830.

The Constitution of the United States guarantees American citizens the right to practice their religious convictions in freedom. For the Saints, though, winning that right proved difficult. Their faith put the guarantee of religious freedom to a test that lasted for decades. Some saw the church as one that preached heresy (something outside of accepted religious beliefs), or saw it as an economic threat. Many of the church's early persecutors were Christian ministers whose own congregation members were leaving to join the new church, led by its charismatic young founder, Joseph Smith.

What inspired so many early Americans to either embrace Joseph Smith's message or despise it? Smith offered some very new ideas on God and humankind, spelled out in *The Book of Mormon,* his book that he claimed was inspired by God. The book tells of an ancient band of Israelites that fled the Holy Land and went to Central America six hundred years before the birth of Jesus of Nazareth. Smith had plans to build a new Zion, or kingdom of God, in America, as he felt ordained to do by God. The plan called for a strict adherence to community living which would help the Mormons prosper financially wherever they went.

Their new ideas, combined with their economic success and devoted loyalty to Joseph Smith, often made the Latter-day Saints outcasts. In the church's first twenty years Smith led his church members from western New York as they attempted to settle themselves in Ohio, Missouri, and Illinois. Each time, they were violently expelled from their settlements by angry neighbors. Their last move was from an Illinois city, Nauvoo, which they built from a swamp on the Mississippi River. The Saints made this move without their "Prophet," as Joseph was called. He had been murdered, and church enemies believed that without its leader the church would scatter.

One of Joseph's most loyal assistants, Brigham Young, demonstrated his leadership skills when he had to move thousands of Saints out of Illinois and across the Mississippi River in mid-winter. He held the church together and led members across the prairies to the desolate Salt Lake Valley, which was unclaimed land in the Great Basin, an arid region ringed halfway around by the Wasatch Mountains. Brigham Young became the second man to hold the titles of Prophet and President of the Church of Jesus Christ of Latter-day Saints. Under his leadership, which ended after three decades in 1877, the Saints turned the parched Great Salt Lake Valley into a desert oasis.

Church converts from Europe poured into the Salt Lake Valley in the mid-1800s, and Mormon-built Salt Lake City became an important economic and cultural center in the West as that part of the country was being settled by white Americans and immigrants. But the Latter-day Saints still had to battle for a place in mainstream America.

What was it about them that people found so hard to accept? There had been other religious groups established in the United States as well as those that came from Europe; different religious denominations became used to living side by side in large and small communities. The Mormons, however, had to flee to an uninhabited part of the country to survive. The Latter-day Saints have always considered themselves Christians, or believers that Jesus Christ was the divine son of God and the savior of the human race. From there, though, much of their faith has little in common with that of other Christians, and their beliefs are based on what were considered to be the God-inspired revelations of Joseph Smith.

The Latter-day Saints believe that the Bible is the word of God, for example, but they also believe *The Book of Mormon* equally important and inspired. They teach that God was once a human being, that there are many other worlds headed by such figures, and that people, by closely following church teachings, also can become gods and, in fact, rule over their own individual planets.

Non-Mormons might have tolerated these religious differences, but what made them angry was the economic system Smith put into practice when a new settlement was begun. He called it the "Law of Consecration," under which all property owned by church members was deeded to the church, then divided and deeded back to all members according to their needs and abilities. Church members patronized one another's businesses, often to the exclusion of non-Mormon business owners, which caused resentment. The Latter-day Saints befriended Native Americans, thinking them to be descendants of the Israelites that were described in *The Book of Mormon* while other white Americans thought of the Indians as sometimes hostile competitors for available land. And the Mormons, though a law-abiding group in general, weren't always very subtle in telling others about their belief that Latter-day Saints were God's chosen people, destined to inherit America.

Only a few years after the Mormons settled in Salt Lake City, they were again engulfed in controversy. Brigham Young shocked the nation when he announced that the Church of Jesus Christ of

Latter-day Saints, as part of its religious beliefs, practiced polygamy, which they called "plural marriage." It was a practice that prevented the Utah Territory, of which Brigham Young was the first governor, from joining the United States as a state, and it caused disagreement within the church as well.

Whatever public relations problems the Latter-day Saints had, they also had a quality that other churches at times envy—a strong sense of unity and a firm belief in the truth of their religion. Today, with the practice of polygamy behind them and Latter-day Saint church districts established in 150 different countries and territories, their faith has brought them far. That faith had its start in 1820 in a small community of western New York, where a teenage boy asked a simple question of God. The answer he received is still being spread throughout the world today.

EARLY PERSECUTION, EARLY FLIGHT

2

On a beautiful spring day in 1820, fourteen-year-old Joseph Smith headed for a favorite grove of trees. Inspired by a passage in the Bible, he hoped to render his mind as clear as the bright blue sky. He was driven there by a desire to better know God. All around his community in western New York, men were attempting to win converts to one form of Christianity or another. These evangelistic revivals had been going on for many years. Joseph attended some of the meetings held by the various preachers, but he only felt lost. As he described it later, "so great were the confusions and strife among the different denominations, that it was impossible" for him to decide who to believe.[1]

Young Joseph did hear some valuable advice from one of the ministers, who quoted a Bible passage from the Book of James that said those with questions about faith should seek wisdom from God. So Joseph sought a quiet and secluded grove of trees. "I kneeled down and began to offer up the desires of my heart to God," he

recalled later in his book *Pearl of Great Price.* "Immediately I was seized upon by some power which entirely overcame me," a power that he later described as a vision of God and Jesus, standing above him in brilliant light.[2] Joseph asked them which of the religious sects he should join, and he was told to join none of them.

Joseph soon discovered that nobody outside of his family wanted to hear of his vision. One preacher who heard him talk about it treated him "with great contempt," and told him visions and revelations from God were impossible.[3] But Joseph was sure of what he had seen, and his family became convinced of it, too.

Like many of their neighbors, the Smiths, a hard-working family originally from New England, were attracted to the fertile soil and milder climate of western New York. Lucy and Joseph Smith, Sr., and their ten children spent several years clearing and cultivating the 100 acres (40 ha) of farmland they'd bought in Palmyra, New York. Joseph, Jr., their fourth child and third son, was known as an outgoing and good-natured young man, which didn't change even as he faced ridicule when word of his vision spread among the community.

Joseph continued his otherwise ordinary life for another few years. While in prayer in his room one evening, at the age of seventeen, he asked God's forgiveness of his tendency to spend his free time in "jovial company," as he called it.[4] Like his prayer in the grove of trees in 1820, this one was answered with a vision. He was visited by

---

Young Joseph Smith was confused by the many religious denominations struggling for power in the early 1800s. He went to this grove of trees in Palmyra, New York, to pray for guidance. He claimed to have a vision of God and Jesus, who told him not to follow others.

Joseph Smith said the angel Moroni told him how to find the gold plates that contained a history of early communities of people in the Americas. This painting shows Joseph holding the plates as he is visited by a vision of Moroni.

an angel calling himself Moroni and whose presence lit the darkened room as if it were midday, as Joseph described it in *Pearl of Great Price*. Moroni told Joseph how to find a book buried nearby, written on thin gold plates. These plates contained information, never revealed to Christians before, compiled by Moroni's father, a fifth century A.D. prophet named Mormon. Smith named *The Book of Mormon* after this prophet, and its believers derived their name from his.

Joseph visited the site Moroni spoke of, called Hill Cumorah, and found the gold plates. They were inscribed with beautiful ancient lettering called "reformed Egyptian." Buried alongside the plates was an ancient interpreting mechanism, called the Urim and the Thummin, for deciphering the reformed Egyptian letters. It consisted of two stones fastened to a breastplate by silver bows. Moroni had told Joseph to leave the plates but return to the site each year

An example of the "Reformed Egyptian" lettering that Joseph claimed he translated from the gold plates

on September 22 for four more years. Moroni would give Joseph the plates after the last visit.

Joseph spent the next four years working to help pay family debts, and visiting Hill Cumorah each year, hearing from Moroni about some of God's plans for "the last days of man," as Joseph described it.[5] On his last visit to the hill, he finally took possession of the plates. Joseph, now twenty-one years old and married to Emma Hale, was warned by Moroni to carefully protect them and show them to no one.

Using the Urim and Thummin, Joseph began translating the golden plates. A blanket hung between Joseph and Emma, and she wrote down what he read. They were living with Joseph's family, and soon interruptions from curious neighbors made work difficult. Emma's father, Isaac Hale, offered the young couple a small house on his property in nearby Harmony, Pennsylvania. They went there, bringing with their other belongings the gold plates, hidden in a barrel of beans.

A local farmer in Harmony, Martin Harris, heard of Joseph's project and offered to help, acting as a scribe while Joseph translated the plates aloud. They worked together for two months, producing 116 pages of manuscript, which were lost when Harris became over-enthusiastic and showed the pages to others. Joseph said that Moroni took the plates from him for awhile, but that the information in the 116 lost pages was revealed in another part of *The Book of Mormon*. Joseph then received help from Oliver Cowdery, a young schoolteacher boarding at his parents' home. Working feverishly, they finished transcribing *The Book of Mormon* by June 1829.

So what does *The Book of Mormon* say? It describes the history of a group of people living in the Americas from about 600 B.C. to

Joseph Smith (left) hung a curtain between himself and those who wrote down his translations of the plates that comprise The Book of Mormon. *Here Oliver Cowdery serves as scribe.*

A.D. 421. They are descended from a man named Lehi, a Hebrew who was divinely directed to lead his family from Jerusalem to South America. Lehi's descendants then split into two conflicting groups, the Nephites and the Lamanites, named after Lehi's sons Nephi and Laman.

The Nephites were thought to be God's chosen people. They

worked hard and were virtuous. Over time, they became prosperous and highly civilized but in the process lost their beliefs. The Lamanites, who had become nomads, eventually rose up in violence against the Nephites. This story of good people gradually becoming corrupt and deserving of God's punishment echoes the style of many stories in the Old Testament of the Bible. In all, *The Book of Mormon* consists of six books translated from the plates of Nephi, an explanatory section called "The Words of Mormon," and then eight books of the writings of Mormon and Moroni.

Joseph and Oliver traveled to Fayette, New York, to stay with friends of Oliver's, the Whitmer family, who also became enthusiastic about the story told in *The Book of Mormon* and Joseph's other revelations. With *The Book of Mormon* transcribed, Joseph was allowed by Moroni to show the gold plates to three other people: Oliver Cowdery, David Whitmer, and an apologetic Martin Harris all viewed the plates and saw Moroni. Eight other men also saw the plates before Moroni took them back.

Joseph and Oliver baptized each other, then baptized members of the Whitmer family and Joseph's older brother, Hyrum. Their first official church meeting was held on April 6, 1830, in the Whitmers' home. They called themselves the Church of Jesus Christ, and by 1838 the name was revised to Church of Jesus Christ of Latter-day Saints. In the meantime, Martin Harris donated $3,000 to have five thousand copies of *The Book of Mormon* printed. As the church grew, Joseph became known as a prophet, much like those from the Old Testament of the Bible. The correct priesthood had been "restored," Joseph and Oliver taught, and a council of twelve apostles was assigned. Church rules were set as Joseph received revelations from God.

Oliver Cowdery

David Whitmer   *Martin Harris*

After Joseph finished translating The Book of Mormon, *he said the angel Moroni gave him permission to show the gold plates to Oliver Cowdery, Martin Harris, and David Whitmer. All three men signed statements that they did indeed see the plates. Cowdery and Harris had helped Joseph record the book. Whitmer hosted the first meeting of the new church.*

Joseph said that *The Book of Mormon,* with its story of the ancient band of Israelites who fled to the New World, contained all information necessary about how the church was to be structured in modern times. Joseph told his congregation that church rules were to be "agreeable to the laws of our country,"[6] and the basic message of the Church of Jesus Christ was that each person must repent of sins, or suffer.

As converts stepped forward to be baptized and this new religion became more widely known, Joseph found himself in a position of controversy to which he would become accustomed in the following years. In June 1830, with church membership nearing forty people, Joseph was arrested and charged by local authorities with "being a disorderly person, setting the country in an uproar by preaching *The Book of Mormon,*" as stated in an arrest warrant signed by other local ministers.[7] He was acquitted, but it would be the first of many arrests for Joseph. After another run-in with the law, he and Oliver had to flee the area.

Joseph's younger brother, Samuel, was sent to New England to distribute some of the thousands of copies of *The Book of Mormon* that had been printed. Samuel Smith gave a book to a Methodist preacher named John Green, who showed it to his carpenter brother-in-law, Brigham Young. This introduction would change the course of Young's life, as well as that of the young church. In the meantime, Oliver began preaching full time and Emma again was Joseph's scribe as he continued his revelations. One of these revela-

The title page of the first edition of The Book of Mormon

THE

BOOK OF MORMON:

AN ACCOUNT WRITTEN BY THE HAND OF MORMON, UPON PLATES TAKEN FROM THE PLATES OF NEPHI.

Wherefore it is an abridgment of the Record of the People of Nephi; and also of the Lamanites; written to the Lamanites, which are a remnant of the House of Israel; and also to Jew and Gentile; written by way of commandment, and also by the spirit of Prophesy and of Revelation. Written, and sealed up, and hid up unto the LORD, that they might not be destroyed; to come forth by the gift and power of GOD, unto the interpretation thereof; sealed by the hand of Moroni, and hid up unto the LORD, to come forth in due time by the way of Gentile; the interpretation thereof by the gift of GOD; an abridgment taken from the Book of Ether.

Also, which is a Record of the People of Jared, which were scattered at the time the LORD confounded the language of the people when they were building a tower to get to Heaven: which is to shew unto the remnant of the House of Israel how great things the LORD hath done for their fathers; and that they may know the covenants of the LORD, that they are not cast off forever; and also to the convincing of the Jew and Gentile that JESUS is the CHRIST, the ETERNAL GOD, manifesting Himself unto all nations. And now if there be fault, it be the mistake of men; wherefore condemn not the things of GOD, that ye may be found spotless at the judgment seat of CHRIST.

BY JOSEPH SMITH, JUNIOR,
AUTHOR AND PROPRIETOR.

PALMYRA:

PRINTED BY E. B. GRANDIN, FOR THE AUTHOR.

1830.

tions was Emma's calling by God to collect hymns for the new church.

By September 1830, the church had grown to more than sixty members. Oliver Cowdery and three other members, including a zealous convert named Parley Pratt, who became one of the most effective missionaries among the Saints, were sent west. One of their stops was near Pratt's hometown of Kirtland, in northeastern Ohio. Pratt thought a Christian sect that called itself the Disciples would be attracted to the story in *The Book of Mormon*. Sidney Rigdon, an influential and fiery Disciple preacher, was indeed convinced that what he read in *The Book of Mormon* was true. He was converted, and he brought with him hundreds of other Disciples.

The missionaries continued west on foot, traveling through Ohio, Kentucky, and into Missouri, having preached about Joseph Smith's revelations to thousands along the way. They also sought out Native Americans, as they believed them to be descendants of some of the people written about in *The Book of Mormon*. American Indians received the missionaries with much interest, which stirred up suspicions among whites who thought perhaps some kind of conspiracy was being plotted between Native Americans and members of this new church.

Back in New York, Sidney Rigdon was now Joseph's scribe, taking down his various revelations, of which there were many. Joseph claimed to be receiving from God many "lost" scriptures, such as the Book of Moses, that had been left out of the Bible as Christians knew it. Joseph also felt he was called to revise the existing Bible. In addition, Joseph said, God had plans for the relocation of the church to Kirtland, to which hundreds of new church members were encouraging Joseph and Emma to move. In January 1831, during a

Joseph Smith believed that Native Americans were the descendants of the Hebrew peoples described in The Book of Mormon.

particularly severe winter, Joseph and his pregnant wife (they had lost their first child) put a few of their belongings on a sleigh and left their childhood homes for Ohio. That spring, Emma gave birth to twins, a boy and a girl, who lived only a few hours. She and Joseph then adopted the infant twins of a nearby man whose wife had died during childbirth.

Following Joseph and Emma's example, other Saints from the northeast began moving to Kirtland, which was a small town of about one thousand people. Many people arrived penniless, relying on the generosity of other Saints for food and housing. It was because of this that Joseph established the groundwork of community living that would sustain the Saints in all of their moves. Such communal help required the cooperation of his church members, of course, who gave some of their land and money to the church to be redistributed to other members in need.

So in two years church membership grew from dozens of people to more than one thousand, and converts were still being won. One reason for the church's rapid growth was its message. At that time a common theme of many Christian groups was that the world as we know it would soon end. Joseph's unusual revelations and proclamations about God sparked additional interest in his church, and his preaching, which improved as he went along, was effective.

Converts streamed into Kirtland expecting to see a stern, intimidating prophet. They were surprised, instead, to meet, as one convert described him in a journal, "a friendly cheerful pleasant agreeable man. I could not help liking him."[8] Joseph was said to hold crowds spellbound as he spoke for hours. He and Emma were always as generous with their food, money, and home as they expected other church members to be. Emma nursed sick church members

Emma Hale Smith, wife of Joseph Smith

through epidemics, and she and Joseph often took in orphans of recently deceased Latter-day Saints.

Many people reported receiving signs from God that they were to join this new church, and Joseph was said to perform various healings. New arrivals to Kirtland were given a place to live, food to eat, and some type of work to perform. Strong community feelings helped hold the church together, even when opposition became fierce.

But as Joseph became more popular, he also began gaining enemies both outside of and within the church. One church member, Ezra Booth, decided Joseph was too light-hearted to be a true prophet of God, and that his revelations occurred too conveniently. Booth and some young men whose parents had become church members (the sons feared their inheritance from their parents would all be given to the church) stirred up enough fear and resentment from others in the Kirtland community to get a mob together that attacked Joseph at his home one Saturday evening in March 1832. Joseph was dragged outside, beaten, and tarred and feathered. Emma had to flee the house with their two sick children, one of whom died shortly after. Sidney Rigdon received similar treatment at his home that night. He was pulled by his feet over the frozen ground, resulting in head injuries that kept him in a semiconscious state for days. Joseph wasn't intimidated, however, and he appeared the next morning on the front porch to deliver his sermon. Several of the mob members who came for him the night before eventually had a change of heart and were baptized.

By that time the church had begun a move to Missouri, where several missionaries, including Oliver Cowdery, then lived. Missouri, Joseph told church members, had been revealed to him by God as Zion, the place where Saints were to gather while awaiting God's final judgment. He collected money from church members and began buying land there. In 1831, a site for a temple was dedicated in Independence, Missouri. Cowdery led the church in Missouri, and the Latter-day Saints began publishing a newspaper there.

Some residents of Kirtland, Ohio, became nervous about Joseph Smith's increasing popularity. This illustration shows them dragging Smith from his home in 1832 and covering him in tar and feathers, a traditional form of persecution.

A temple was planned for Kirtland as well, and building began in 1833. It was built by church members, and women wove rugs for the interior and donated glassware and china to be ground into a sparkling plaster for the outside walls. By now, Joseph had been named President of the High Priesthood, a position often referred to as church president, and he was assisted by two Counselors. The Quorum of Twelve Apostles, who were to spread the restored gospel as missionaries, also contributed to church-making decisions. One of the twelve, Brigham Young, had become a good friend to and devoted follower of Joseph.

Problems developed, however, as the church moved forward in its organizational structure and plans to build temples. Missionaries were winning converts from Missouri to New England, but in their Zion (Jackson County, Missouri) the Saints were having troubles with non-Mormon neighbors. Some of their differences were cultural: most of the Saints moving there were from northern states and were anti-slavery, welcoming free African-Americans as church members. Most other white Missourians were pro-slavery southerners. The Mormons considered Native Americans to be descendants of the Lamanites, a group of people mentioned in *The Book of Mormon,* and were friendly with them, but Missourians distrusted the Indians. Joseph had a city plan he had designed for Independence printed in the Mormon newspaper, and non-Mormons began to view the Saints as a potential threat. Violence against the Saints erupted with vandalism and the destruction of their printing press in 1833. Mobs also went from house to house, forcing Mormon families out and setting the homes on fire.

By 1834, Latter-day Saints had left Jackson County and spread out into neighboring communities. Joseph led what he called the Armies of Israel to Missouri to help. Upon arriving, however, most of his "soldiers" battled cholera instead, leaving fourteen dead. Joseph returned to Ohio with Saints scattered about the area, but eventually the church established a settlement that was named Far West. Life for the Saints quieted down for awhile, and missionaries were sent to England.

Joseph Smith had a city plan for Kirtland, too, where the Saints had become the main political power. But between building a temple and buying land in Missouri, the Mormons had little cash with which to build a city. In the fall of 1836, Joseph and other church leaders put a bank plan into action. They ended up with what they called an "anti-banking" company, since they were denied permission from the state to open an actual bank. They issued money (which was legal for banks to do in those days) to church members, who then discovered they were unable to spend it at non-Mormon businesses. Then even the bank itself, to keep from failing, refused to take the money. Joseph tried to save the "anti-bank" by borrowing money and selling land, but his plan didn't work. Kirtland's economy became based on credit and the money from the anti-bank that no one wanted.

As Joseph scrambled to try to salvage the local economy, his reputation began to suffer as well. Non-Mormons in northeast Ohio had been hammering away at him for awhile, such as the editor of the *Painesville Telegraph,* who dug up any information about Joseph that would make him appear bad. When the Mormon bank went bad, even Latter-day Saints within Joseph's inner circle began to consider Joseph a fallen prophet, and because of threats on his life Joseph had to leave town frequently. Then there were the rumors that only made matters worse for Joseph in his position of leadership: it was said that he had formed some new ideas on marriage and was sometimes linked to relationships with women other than his wife.

Mormons think Joseph's "revelation" about polygamy, or plural marriages, as the Latter-day Saint church refers to it, came about when he was revising the Bible in the early 1830s. The church teaches that Joseph asked God why plural wives were accepted in ancient Biblical times (to such patriarchs as Abraham and Isaac), but not in modern times. One purpose of the Latter-day Saints was to restore the "church" that it believed had always existed but was lost in the centuries after Jesus' death and resurrection. Polygamy, which the Saints called "the principle," was one more element of the ancient church that Joseph was required by God to restore, Latter-day Saints believe, though among church members it caused serious disagreement for years.

Joseph's biggest problem in Kirtland was the charge of fraud; he and Sidney Rigdon fled the town on horseback. Even Oliver Cowdery, David Whitmer, and Martin Harris, three who had been with him the longest, spoke out against Joseph, and all three left the church. Brigham Young was forced to flee because he still supported Joseph.

Joseph and Brigham and their families headed for Missouri, followed by angry mobs for 200 miles (322 km). But they arrived safely and received a warm greeting from the Saints in Far West. Most church members in Kirtland remained loyal, too, and many eventually moved west. When Joseph arrived in the mid-1830s, Far West was a community of about 1,500, in addition to the Saints scattered in a few other communities. With Joseph's move there, the Mormon population began to increase. Joseph renewed his plans for a big city and spoke of the greatness the Saints would achieve. Once again, their non-Mormon neighbors began to get nervous.

On July 4, 1837, the Saints had a public demonstration of their military readiness to defend themselves, and Sidney Rigdon gave a speech about a "war of extermination."[9] His speech was published in a local paper, and Saints living outside the Far West area had to go there for protection from mob beatings and destruction of property.

This time the Mormons fought back, and small battles erupted. By October 1838, Missouri Governor Lilburn Boggs had received reports such as the one that told him, "We know not the hour or minute we will be laid in ashes" at the hands of the Saints. He was alarmed, so he told a state militia general to consider the Mormons enemies of the state. He even gave the militia permission to "exterminate" Mormons, or at least drive them from the state.[10]

On October 30, an armed mob attacked a small settlement at Haun's Mill on the eastern boundary of Caldwell County. While women and children ran into the woods, a group of men, which included a few boys, tried to take cover in a log cabin. Shooting through the gaps between the logs and finally breaking into the cabin, the mob killed nineteen men and boys.

The next day, Joseph Smith and Sidney Rigdon surrendered to the local militia and were imprisoned for months. Zion appeared to be falling apart: church leaders were imprisoned, or they rebelled against Joseph, while loyal Saints were being driven from their homes as winter approached. Straight to the east, across the Mississippi River, residents of Quincy, Illinois, sympathized with the Mormons and offered them hospitality and help. The Saints were down, but another chapter of the greatness of which Joseph spoke was soon to come.

Heber C. Kimball helped the Mormons escape from persecution in Missouri and became an important church leader. He also holds the record for plural marriages, with forty-three wives.

TO NAUVOO

After Governor Boggs gave his militia permission to "exterminate" the Mormons, Missouri vigilantes chased the remaining Saints out of Missouri. Brigham Young and the friend he'd brought with him to the church, Heber C. Kimball, weren't recognized. They stayed behind to get everybody out. But by mid-February in 1839, Young was a wanted man, and he fled. Kimball remained to finish the job.

By April most Saints had made it to Quincy, where residents helped with material aid and jobs for the men. There was even a "welcome" from Illinois Governor Thomas Carlin. That month, Joseph was allowed to "escape" from jail in Missouri. He soon joined his family on the other side of the river.

Joseph found an area about 50 miles (80 km) upriver surrounded on three sides by the Mississippi and decided it would be a good spot for a city. At the time it was just a mosquito-ridden, malaria-infected swamp. Nevertheless, the Saints began moving there to establish the city Joseph named Nauvoo, a Hebrew word meaning "beautiful."

Missionary trips to England didn't miss a beat, although leading missionaries such as Brigham Young had to leave behind families ill with malaria. Young himself was sick and barely able to walk. But their efforts would be rewarded with thousands of English converts who would move to Nauvoo in the next few years.

Joseph began buying land and seeking the friendship of local politicians. Since Mormons tended to vote as the church suggested and represented thousands of votes to officeholders, politicians sought their friendship as well. But politicians in Washington, D.C., weren't as friendly. Joseph had an audience with U.S. President Martin Van Buren in 1839, hoping the federal government would address the treatment that the Mormons received at the hands of the Missourians. The president offered Joseph a little sympathy, but nothing else, and Joseph's plea before members of Congress got the same result. To make matters worse, Missouri Governor Boggs was angered that Joseph had advertised the Mormon-Missouri conflict before a national audience; Joseph would be hearing from his old enemies before long.

When a new convert, John C. Bennett, arrived at Nauvoo in 1840, it was a town of about three thousand people. His stay was not long, but it was influential. Bennett claimed to have backgrounds in medicine, law, and religious ministry. He showed the Saints how to drain the swampland, a process that relieved them of much of the deadly malaria. Bennett's most important contribution, though, was a city charter, or government plan, that he drew up. It allowed Nauvoo its own militia and court system.

Unusual as that was, Bennett brought the city charter to the state legislature in Springfield. Dangling the prospect of Mormon votes before the state politicians, he won approval of the charter. Now Joseph could act on his plans for a university, a library, and a music hall. John Bennett was elected mayor of Nauvoo.

Nauvoo grew quickly. By 1841, the swampland had become a city of 1,500 buildings, with more always under construction. Building material came from church-owned timber camps in Wisconsin. A site for a temple was dedicated, and its construction became a priority.

Church doctrine also grew, as Joseph's revelations continued. "Awake, O kings of the earth! Come ye . . . with your gold and silver to the help of my people" was one such revelation, telling Latter-day converts to gather in Nauvoo to help in the temple building.[1]

Another revelation told of a new temple ordinance, or church ceremony, that Joseph said was essential—baptism for the dead, which Mormons still practice today. Joseph told the Saints that their ancestors who died before knowing about this restored church of Jesus Christ could reside in even higher glory in Heaven if their descendants underwent baptism for them. Because of this belief, genealogy, or the tracing of one's "family tree," has become very important to Latter-day Saints.

Joseph told the Saints that only tithing church members (those who give one-tenth of their income to the church) could take part in temple ordinances. He taught the church that there are many worlds in the universe as well as many gods. The God of Earth, who used to be a human being, is just one of many. Those who live especially holy lives can look forward to becoming gods themselves and ruling over their own worlds. "As man is, God once was. As God is, man may become" is a favorite Mormon saying.

Also, after many years of rumors, Joseph finally began unveiling to church counselors and apostles his revelation on polygamy, though publicly he denied it. He had been called upon by God to restore all valid ancient customs, and God had made it clear, Joseph told them, that polygamy was one of those practices. Even those closest to him, such as his brother Hyrum and Sidney Rigdon, were shocked, and Rigdon left Nauvoo for Pittsburgh. When the twelve apostles returned from their missions in England they, too, learned of what would become a command for church leaders and found it hard to believe.

Monogamy, or marriage to only one spouse, had been an unquestioned Judeo-Christian tradition. The ancient practice of polygamy was, in their minds, like adultery, or something "savages" would practice. But as Brigham thought about it, he realized he already loved two wives—his first, who had died, and his second, upon remarriage. He came to accept it and helped Joseph convince the other apostles to embrace it, too.

Joseph waited until he had already "married" other women before telling his wife Emma of this "ancient" principle. She was president of the recently formed Nauvoo Relief Society, a Mormon women's organization designed to help Saints in need. She probably wasn't aware that Joseph had married two of her co-Relief Society members. Emma never did accept polygamy.

Not everyone was to practice polygamy. Permission to do so, usually in the form of a strong suggestion, came from Joseph. John Bennett hadn't received permission to take on plural wives, but he used his position in the town and church to try to convince various women that he was "commanded" to take them as wives. Bennett was excommunicated from the church in 1842 and gave aid to

Brigham Young proved an able leader who would become the leader of the church after Smith and keep it strong.

Joseph's enemies in the area, such as newspaper editor Thomas Sharp. Sharp saw Joseph as a power-hungry empire builder and wrote about the Mormon "threat" in his newspaper, the Warsaw *Signal*.

Joseph had already been arrested and put on trial at the request of Governor Boggs of Missouri. The trial was also supported by Illinois Governor Carlin, who had cooled toward the Mormons. Other warrants issued for Joseph's arrest kept him a frequent fugitive from the law. In 1843, with testimony from John Bennett, a grand jury indicted Joseph on grounds of treason against the United States, because Joseph had used his militia to defend the Saints during their Missouri persecution. Treason—breaking one's allegiance against the country in which one lives—was and remains a very serious crime, and is the only crime defined in the U.S. Constitution.

This time, Joseph was captured. Though he was freed later in the year, it made him aware that the Mormons might not be any safer in Illinois than they were in Missouri. Scouts were sent west to look for an area to which the Saints might eventually move, and Joseph was especially interested in the Rocky Mountains.

By 1843, Nauvoo had become the largest city in Illinois, as converts and English immigrants swelled the population to twenty thousand. Joseph, Emma, and their children lived in a large home that included rooms to rent. In the summer, the Smiths hosted festive riverboat parties with music and dancing.

But even as Nauvoo enjoyed prosperity, Joseph was beginning to feel increasing pressure from outside and within the church. It was getting harder to keep the state politicians happy. Both prominent political parties of the day, the Whigs and Democrats, competed for Mormon votes. Non-Mormons saw the increasing population of Nauvoo as an attempt to eventually control the state. Though most of the Saints continued to be devoted followers of Joseph, some of those closest to him were having second thoughts about his leadership, especially when Joseph introduced polygamy.

Nevertheless, as the 1844 presidential election year drew closer, and no candidate was willing to promise the Mormons protection, Joseph decided to become a candidate for U.S. president himself. His platform contained ideas that most politicians even today would be afraid to say aloud, such as reducing the number of congressmen by two-thirds. By paying fewer members of Congress and selling federal land, Joseph proposed that government pay southerners for their slaves and abolish slavery. In general, he favored fewer taxes, less federal government, and more equality among people. Mormon missionaries spread his platform along with church doctrine.

From within the church, anti-polygamy members were opposing what Joseph stood for, at least as the leader of the Latter-day Saints. William Law, one of Joseph's two counselors, broke away and formed his own church based on *The Book of Mormon*. Like the early Mormon church, this new religion used a newspaper to present its views. But this anti-Smith newspaper, the *Nauvoo Expositor*, made its first and last appearance in June 1844.

Joseph, who had replaced John Bennett as mayor of Nauvoo, met with the city council and declared the new newspaper a public nuisance. Its presses were confiscated and destroyed (as had happened to Mormon presses in Missouri). Joseph may have thought this was within the rights of the city government, but others outside Nauvoo didn't agree. The nearby Warsaw *Signal* ran a headline that read "WAR." Also, Joseph was wanted on a charge of inciting a riot.

Harassment began for Saints living outside Nauvoo. Expecting another serious conflict, Joseph called the missionary apostles back home and advised his brother Hyrum to send their families by steamboat to Cincinnati. "Joseph, I can't leave you," Hyrum replied.[2] They decided instead to flee together, crossing the river into Iowa, with the intention of finding a safe place for the Saints in the West.

Joseph wept as he bade Emma and their children good-bye before he and Hyrum were rowed across the Mississippi. But Joseph was stung by criticism from leading loyal church members, such as Heber Kimball, who called Joseph a coward for leaving. Hyrum, too, wanted to return. Reluctantly, Joseph agreed, but, he warned Hyrum, "we shall be butchered."[3]

They surrendered in nearby Carthage on June 24 and were jailed the next day, along with the two remaining apostles in town. The jail was "guarded" by an anti-Mormon militia; on the evening of June 27, a mob gathered outside the building and stormed it. Shots were fired outside and inside the jail, and a group of men broke down the door of the room where Joseph, Hyrum, John Taylor, and Willard Richards were kept. Hyrum was shot and killed immediately, and as Joseph jumped through the second-story window he was shot from outside and inside the jail, falling dead to the ground. Taylor was seriously wounded. Richards, only nicked by a bullet, was able to send word to Nauvoo about the killings.

After years of conflict, the dynamic leader of the Church of Jesus Christ of Latter-day Saints was dead, and church enemies thought the church would die, too. The people of Nauvoo grieved heavily over the deaths of Joseph and Hyrum. But there also was much faith, and, in Brigham Young, an equally strong leader ready to take the reins of the growing church and lead it further still.

Joseph Smith was being held in this jail (in rear of picture) in Carthage, Illinois, when a mob forced their way in and shot him as he fell from the second floor window. The man with the blackened face is being stopped from mutilating the body of the slain Smith; he and others in the mob colored their faces to avoid identification in the unlawful act of murdering Smith. Hyrum Smith, who was also killed in the attack, is being carried off in the left of this picture.

BRIGHAM YOUNG LEADS MORMONS WEST

4

efore dawn on June 28, 1844, the cries of Porter Rockwell, a devoted friend and follower of Joseph Smith, broke the morning stillness as he galloped through Nauvoo. "Joseph is killed—they have killed him! Goddam them! They have killed him!"[1]

Official notice of the deaths of Joseph and Hyrum Smith came in a letter that morning from Willard Richards to Emma Smith. The letter said Carthage residents were promised there would be no retaliation from the Mormons, and that Taylor, who didn't want to worry his family, was slightly wounded. Emma then urged the townspeople to "remain quiet and peaceable."

A brass band accompanied the bodies of Joseph and Hyrum back into town. They were buried in a secret place to foil grave robbers (there was a bounty on Joseph's head, dead or alive). For awhile, a strange calm fell over the area. The Saints, and the Nauvoo militia, awaited further attacks that didn't come.

No clear line of leadership succession for the Saints had been established. Willard Richards and John Taylor were the only apostles in town, and Richards ran the church while Taylor recovered from his gunshot wounds. The other apostles were called back immediately from their mission work; in the meantime, Sidney Rigdon heard of the situation and arrived in Nauvoo in early August.

When Brigham Young arrived a few days later, he found Rigdon claiming authority from Joseph and from God to assume church leadership. Rigdon preached long and hard to members about his rightful authority and about the bloody revenge the Mormons would take on their enemies. Brigham calmly proposed that the Quorum of Twelve, of which he was president, run the church for the time being. With a show of hands, the membership chose to put their lives in the hands of the church apostles. Some members even claimed to see Brigham transfigured into Joseph Smith while he was speaking. Rigdon, bitter in spirit, was excommunicated from the church shortly after.

It wasn't so easily settled for all church members, though. Anti-polygamists, who counted Emma Smith among them, claimed Joseph was ready to give up "the principle" at the time of his death. James Strang, who had been sent to Wisconsin to look for a potential settlement area for the Saints, and William Marks, who was president of the Nauvoo stake, both wanted a Mormon church without polygamy. Thousands of Saints, including Joseph's mother, Lucy, followed Strang when he founded such a church.

But most of the church membership stayed with the apostles. Polygamy was a sore issue for many, especially for wives of men who practiced it, but in Nauvoo it directly affected only about thirty families. Joseph Smith is believed to have had twenty-seven wives at the

Brigham Young and some of his twenty-seven wives

time of his death, though few of them used his name. If any children were born to those wives, none used the Smith name. Hyrum's wife, Mary Fielding Smith, became a plural wife of Heber C. Kimball, who held the official church record for plural marriages with forty-three wives. By the end of the year of Joseph's death, Brigham had taken an additional six wives. He also married eight of Joseph's plural widows, and eventually had twenty-seven wives, the same number as Joseph Smith.

Polygamy was expected of prominent church members. Publicly, Joseph Smith told his general membership that without marriage, a man wouldn't be able to achieve the highest glory possible in Heaven. Privately, Smith told his apostles that the more wives they took, the higher that level of glory would be. One woman who didn't see it as anything glorious was Brigham Young's sister-in-law, who wrote in a letter from Nauvoo, "With a sad heart I found all the married people at liberty to choose new companions if they so desired."[2]

Emma Smith remained staunchly opposed to polygamy. Emma and Joseph's oldest son, Joseph Smith III, eventually headed a smaller church, the Reorganized Church of Jesus Christ of Latter Day Saints. This church eliminated many Latter-day Saint doctrines and practices, such as baptism for the dead and especially polygamy, but kept *The Book of Mormon*, still considering it to be divinely inspired. It is their church property in Independence, Missouri, that contains the graves of Joseph and Hyrum Smith.

Most Latter-day Saints accepted polygamy, whether they liked it or not, as a commandment from God that didn't affect many church members. In 1845, the Saints were more worried about survival than doctrine. During the winter, the Illinois legislature had repealed the Nauvoo city charter, leaving its court system powerless and its militia illegal. Anti-Mormon vigilantes began attacking Saints in and outside of Nauvoo.

By autumn 1845, church leaders promised state officials they would head west the following spring. At the twice-yearly church conference that fall, the nearly five thousand church members attending were told to begin saving food and prepare for a spring-time westward migration, even as converts continued to arrive from England. Saints worked constantly to finish the Nauvoo Temple so they could leave on their journey properly endowed, or specially blessed. This, however, made the local non-Mormons think they weren't really leaving: why would the Mormons work so hard on the temple just to leave it behind? Attacks on the Saints increased.

By February there were reports that the apostles, still led by Brigham Young, could be arrested at any time, and a decision was made to leave Nauvoo immediately. During the first week of February 1846, wagons began crossing the frozen Mississippi River, and camps were set up in Lee County, Iowa. Though most Mormons were ill prepared for the sudden departure, the river crossings continued day and night.

Nine babies were born during the first night's rainy encampment, one in a tent so leaky that attending women spent the night keeping the mother and infant dry by catching water in pots and pans. Many of those coming to Iowa had only enough food for a few days and were helped by those Saints who came better prepared.

In all, about four hundred wagons gathered to continue west over the Iowa plains, hoping to make it to the Rocky Mountains that year, while a few hundred families stayed in Lee County to grow food. Some traveled through the winter storms in uncovered wagons, and deaths from exposure were common. Eventually the apostles organized the Saints into two large groups, and then into groups of one hundred each. These groups were subdivided into groups of two fifties and then tens, with officers over each. Food and supplies were distributed among each group of fifty.

Traveling proved slow and difficult, and an advance party went ahead to find a place where a temporary settlement could be made to grow food and prepare for the rest of the journey. By June, just across the Missouri River near present-day Omaha, Nebraska, the wagon trains came to a halt, and plans for a temporary "city" were made. Joining it was another settlement on the Iowa side of the river in what is today Council Bluffs. The Potawatomi Indian tribe agreed to let the Mormons remain on the land, and the settlements came to be called Winter Quarters.

As the Saints traveled to Winter Quarters, a United States Army captain caught up with them and requested five hundred men to help fight the Mexican War. Though it was hard to spare them, Brigham Young agreed. In addition to the food, uniforms, and monthly pay the men would receive, the army gave the Saints money up front in exchange for the men, which would be helpful. They would be discharged from California the following year and could help scout out new land in the West. More than five hundred men went. The army paymaster was surprised when, on the first payday, each member of the "Mormon Battalion" was able to sign his name, an unusual accomplishment for that era.

In the meantime, a city was emerging on the Nebraska prairie. Homes were built, wells were dug, and land was cleared for farming. There was much work to be done, but Brigham wanted it done cheerfully. At the end of each day there was singing, dancing, and socializing, and the camp population grew as thousands of Saints continued to arrive after being chased out of Nauvoo.

A makeshift collection of log cabins, huts, and homes dug out of the hills sheltered the Saints as they prepared to travel again the next year. Children attended school and thousands of acres were

The Mormon Battalion

farmed. In spite of a 15 percent death rate from scurvy (a disease caused by a lack of vitamin C) that winter, missionaries continued their trips to England. An English group of musicians, who had emigrated, provided music for the dances that helped distract the Saints from their difficult circumstances.

During the winter of 1846–47, Brigham was envisioning the

Great Salt Lake Valley, 1,000 miles (1,600 km) west, as the most likely destination for the Saints. In this parched and desolate land, there was no one to bother the Saints, and the conditions would make them dependent on God.

As the prairie snows melted in early April, Brigham led an advance party of twenty-five wagons west. Included in this group were three women, two children, three African-American church members from Mississippi, and two non-Mormons. They broke a trail on the north side of the Platte River, trying to avoid a party of Missourians traveling on the Oregon Trail south of the river. Much of their trail would eventually be used by the Union Pacific Railroad.

More than three months later, lying in the back of a wagon and sick with "mountain fever," Brigham looked upon the valley as they came through a mountain canyon and declared, "This is the place, drive on."[3]

DESERET

5

y the time Brigham Young was gazing upon the valley that would become Salt Lake City, camp had already been established there. Some Saints, including the scholarly Orson Pratt, who took daily temperature readings along the way and kept track of barometer readings to estimate their increasing altitude, were already at work damming a stream to soften the sun-baked dirt. Within a few days several acres were plowed and seeded with potatoes, corn, winter wheat, and other crops.

On Sunday, July 25, 1847, the Saints held a worship service, thankful for arriving with no loss of life. Though still ill, Brigham did have some spiritual and practical advice for them. There should be no working or hunting on Sundays. Also, trees were scarce, so only dead trees should be used for firewood. No one would buy land; rather, the church would parcel it out to individual families according to their needs and abilities. After exploring the area, it was determined that their camp was in the best spot for a new

In the 1840s and 1850s, thousands of Mormon settlers crossed the Great Plains to settle in the area around Salt Lake City.

settlement. The land was dry and treeless, but there was water for irrigation.

While on the trek west, they had risen each day to a 5:00 A.M. bugle call. After prayers, cooking, eating, and feeding the animal teams, another bugle call at 7:00 A.M. meant it was time to go. Some of the Indian tribes they encountered were troublesome, burning off grass on the north side of the river to discourage the Saints, or stealing horses at night. Mormon men walked with their rifles alongside the wagons during the day and kept a watch by night. But most of the Native Americans were friendly and sometimes gave the Saints provisions.

They wrote several dozen letters that were carried back to Winter Quarters by a helpful fur trapper. Knowing more Saints would be on the way, they left notes at prominent spots for those coming along the trail, and even turned sun-parched buffalo skulls into "mailboxes."

Upon reaching Fort Laramie in present-day Wyoming, this first pioneer party met up with another party of Saints from Mississippi who had come by way of Pueblo. Here the whole group needed to cross the river and turn south. They hired a boat to take them across and were told by the boat owner that they had just missed Lilburn Boggs and his group headed for Oregon. In June, 142 miles (228 km) from Fort Laramie, the Saints overtook the Missourians and were even paid by their old enemies to be ferried across the Platte.

At one point that summer, Samuel Brannan, who had traveled by boat with a group of New York Saints to California, met up with the wagon train. He had a copy of his Mormon newspaper, *The California Star*, to show Brigham Young. Brannan tried to convince Young to take the Saints to the inviting land of California, and was disappointed when Brigham stuck by his revelation to settle amid the Rocky Mountains.

Finally, Young's first party of Saints arrived at the Salt Lake Valley intact. A city was planned—thousands more Saints would be coming! The city was mapped out in 10-acre (4-ha) blocks, and homes would be placed so none were directly across from each other, a model that Joseph Smith had liked for the cities he planned. Everyone would be encouraged to grow shade and fruit trees. Space for four public squares was allotted, and 40 acres (16 ha) in the middle of town were set aside for a temple. The city that had been built on the banks of the Mississippi River and then deserted would soon begin to reappear, this time with mountains for a backdrop and plenty of room to grow. They called this unclaimed territory "Deseret," a word from *The Book of Mormon* meaning "honeybee."

Camp population increased to about four hundred with the return of battalion members, who had recently been discharged (after making the longest infantry march in American history, much of which became the route for the Southern Pacific Railroad). More Mississippi Saints, who had been living in Pueblo, joined the camp as well. Within the first week it was decided to build a stockade to protect livestock from theft by the Shoshone and Ute Indian tribes. The settlers' homes were built into the adobe-brick structure, and more dwellings were added as the population grew. As was usual for the Mormons, a school was established that first winter which, fortunately, turned out to be a mild one.

The first planting was harvested, and in August Brigham proposed the Saints "call this place 'The Great Salt Lake City.'" By month's end, he led a party back over their trail. As they made their way to Winter Quarters, this group would also determine the needs of the oncoming pioneers.

Back in Winter Quarters, late in the fall of 1847, Brigham Young was voted in by the church membership as the second President and Prophet of the church. One of his first actions as president was to send word to all Saints in the United States, Canada, and England to come to Utah and to bring a variety of seeds. Young established Kanesville, the settlement just across the Missouri River from Winter Quarters, as the point at which pioneer Saints would prepare for their westward trek. Missionary efforts for England and Canada were increased. In the next four years, more than 12,000 Saints, half of them from Great Britain, would go through Kanesville on their way to Utah. About half of the Nauvoo Saints eventually made it to Utah.

In the spring of 1848, Brigham Young and Heber Kimball rode at the head of another wagon train, this one made up of more than 600 wagons carrying almost 2,000 people. Soon after, Willard Richards headed a group of 169 wagons with more than 500 people. For the next fifteen years, wagon trains continued to carry Latter-day Saints across the midwest plains.

By 1848, Salt Lake City had three sawmills and one gristmill in operation, and more than 5,000 acres (2,020 ha) farmed by irrigating the land. The Saints were optimistic about their second harvest until, in May, their growing crops were bombarded with swarms of crickets that appeared from over the mountains. Desperate to preserve their winter food supply, the Saints dug water trenches around the fields, lit fires around them, and even tried an army of broom-swatters, all to no avail. After all their effort, however, what was left of the crops was saved when an even bigger flock of seagulls appeared and devoured all the crickets. The Saints, not knowing this was a normal occurrence, thought it was a miracle. Years later, Brigham Young's grandson sculpted the *Seagull Monument,* which was given a prominent place near the temple in Salt Lake City.

This relief sculpture is one of four on the base of the Seagull Monument, sculpted by Brigham Young's grandson. It commemorates the huge flock of seagulls that saved crops in Salt Lake City in 1848 from crickets that were devouring the Mormons' crops.

Also that year, in Kanesville, the Saints accepted one of their original members back into the church when Oliver Cowdery arrived with his family after a ten-year absence. He hoped to go to Utah, and then England as a missionary, but he died in Iowa just two years later.

Under Brigham Young's direction, missionary efforts expanded to other parts of Europe and Latin America, targeting the poor of those continents. The Mormon missionaries who went to other countries taught not just the Latter-day Saints' doctrine, but also about a new society that the Mormons wanted to help build, a society where all worked equally hard to enjoy a decent standard of living. The poor of England and Northern Europe liked that message. The church's biggest missionary successes were in Great Britain and Scandinavia.

The Perpetual Emigrating Fund was established to help converts answer the Prophet's call to come to Utah. The fund was a loan program that stayed in operation for most of the remainder of the century. Without it, Mormon emigration to the United States would have been far less. Almost eleven thousand Scandinavians came to Utah in the fund's first twenty years, for example, but only three thousand were able to do so without a loan from the fund.

Just as the Saints' move from Nauvoo to Winter Quarters and then to Utah were organized and carried out with much planning and efficiency, the European converts had a plan to follow, too.

The church was well organized in its efforts to bring new settlers to Utah. They published the Emigrants' Guide to help travelers navigate the terrain during their westward migration.

THE

LATTER-DAY SAINTS'

EMIGRANTS' GUIDE:

BEING A

TABLE OF DISTANCES,

SHOWING ALL THE

SPRINGS, CREEKS, RIVERS, HILLS, MOUNTAINS,

CAMPING PLACES, AND ALL OTHER NOTABLE PLACES,

FROM COUNCIL BLUFFS,

TO THE

VALLEY OF THE GREAT SALT LAKE.

ALSO, THE

LATITUDES, LONGITUDES AND ALTITUDES

OF THE PROMINENT POINTS ON THE ROUTE.

TOGETHER WITH REMARKS ON THE NATURE OF THE LAND,
TIMBER, GRASS, &c.

THE WHOLE ROUTE HAVING BEEN CAREFULLY MEASURED BY A ROADOME-
TER, AND THE DISTANCE FROM POINT TO POINT, IN
ENGLISH MILES, ACCURATELY SHOWN.

BY W. CLAYTON.

ST. LOUIS:

MO. REPUBLICAN STEAM POWER PRESS—CHAMBERS & KNAPP.
1848.

Emigrant groups organized in their native countries into wards, or church congregations, that stayed together during the entire trip under the direction of a bishop. They were, in effect, a moving village.

Before the railroads provided access to the western territories in the late 1860s, a Mormon emigrant's trip from Liverpool, England, to Salt Lake City took about nine months. Some pioneers had made it out west on foot, pulling handcarts. Brigham Young put that idea into large-scale action in the 1850s with handcart companies, which reduced the cost of the trans-America trip for the poorer Saints. The English converts could make the entire trip for about $45 each. From Kanesville the emigrants could load their belongings into one or more two-wheeled handcarts and walk their way west, sleeping in tents along the way. One disastrous trip occurred when 576 Saints with handcarts left Iowa too late, in mid-July, and were given carts which, made from unseasoned wood, repeatedly broke. The breakdowns slowed them down, and they met with early winter weather. One-fourth of them died along the way.

Groups usually approached Salt Lake City, passing through Emigration Canyon, late in the summer. Newly arrived Saints sometimes even received an escort from Brigham Young himself, who enjoyed greeting the wagon trains as they arrived. The wide-open scenery of Salt Lake City looked beautiful to the newcomers, who had left crowded European cities behind them. New arrivals usually spent their first winter in Utah recuperating from their long trip. Even then, they earned their keep by helping to build schools, churches, or roads. They received their pay in cash or store credit. Perhaps the most important building project was the temple in Salt Lake City. Over its forty-year construction period, much of the temple was completed by these immigrants.

Many settlers used handcarts to transport their possessions west to Utah. The terrain was difficult, and one year many who were caught in winter weather lost their lives.

By spring, new families were assigned to villages throughout the Rocky Mountains. Brigham Young was ensuring that the entire area would be settled by Mormons. "We calculate to be the kings of these mountains," Brigham was reported to have said. "Now let us go ahead and occupy them."[1] The village of St. George, for example, in the southwest corner of Utah, was begun in 1861 when Brigham sent 309 families there. They provided the territory with sugar, grapes, tobacco, almonds, and cotton.

Each family was assigned a plot of land. If they didn't make good use of it, it might be given to another. Each village was a ward in the Salt Lake City Stake, or district, and the ward bishop's job was much like that of a mayor. He watched over the widows and orphans or sick and elderly, he was in charge of all village and church affairs, both business and spiritual, he dealt with the local Native Americans, and he saw to it that schools were established.

In 1850, Utah was organized into a territory of the United States, and Brigham Young served as its first governor. That year the first issues of *The Deseret News* were published. Today it is a major daily newspaper. This time the Mormons were really established, having quickly put together a small empire that couldn't be shaken or destroyed by jealous or irate vigilantes. Even the United States Army would find that out in the first decade of the "Rocky Mountain Empire."

Things had looked bleak when the Saints were freezing and struggling to stay alive through the winter they were chased from Nauvoo. Nevertheless, William Clayton, who had been a secretary to Joseph Smith, had written a hymn that foresaw a better future for the Saints:

> *We'll find the place which God for us prepared,*
> *Far away in the west,*
> *Where none shall come to hurt or make afraid;*
> *There the Saints will be blessed.*[2]

BUILDING A SOCIETY

6

A new civilization was being built from the ground up in the Rocky Mountains, over which one man, Brigham Young, had tight control. As he and Joseph Smith had planned, there were few non-Mormons in the area to complain about it, at least at first. Like any growing community, though, the Mormons began to draw attention and criticism from those around them.

Many Saints, too, disliked the control the church had over their lives. Families were assigned a village to live in, and the more prominent men in the church (those who had successful businesses or were church leaders) were pressured to practice polygamy, which often disrupted a family's domestic harmony. A man ordered away as a missionary might leave behind his struggling pioneer family and not see them for years.

The Saints weren't excommunicated for not obeying "suggestions," and most polygamous men took just one additional wife to

65

please the church. Pressure to conform to village assignments, career changes (to suit the needs of a new village), and plural marriages varied as the church's own circumstances and leadership did.

But Saints also were part of a unique culture that drew them together in a way that few other religions could do. Individual freedom and capitalism were strong tenets, or basic ingredients, of the American culture. The purpose of the Mormons, especially under Joseph Smith and Brigham Young, was to gather together God's people to build Zion (God's kingdom) on earth while awaiting the second coming of Jesus and the final judgment of mankind. This goal found much use for capitalism and economic freedom; once in Utah the Church of the Latter-day Saints gathered much wealth that enabled it to grow steadily.

Saints were expected to give up a certain amount of individual freedom in order to help the church flourish, and many non-Mormons found this threatening. Even though Joseph directed the church to follow the "laws of the land" (before polygamy violated any federal laws), people outside the church still wondered: If they had enough power, would Joseph Smith or Brigham Young try to gain the property or rights of non-Mormons as well?

The church's influence over its members' lives included a good deal of nurturing. Those who made the long journey to Salt Lake City immediately became part of a community that welcomed them, gave them a home, and enabled them to earn a living. While immigrant children living in the slums of big eastern cities such as New York might spend hours each day working in a factory to help support their families, education was a primary part of every Mormon child's life, even when they lived in temporary settlements.

"The glory of God is intelligence," Joseph Smith wrote in *Doctrine of the Covenants.*

African-Americans began joining the church during and after the era of slavery. They did not encounter as much discrimination with the Mormons as they would have in many other churches. (Even so, it wasn't until 1978 that black male LDS church members were finally ordained to the priesthood.)

Brigham frequently visited the villages that he had "planted" to help settle disputes that sometimes arose when families who were strangers to each other suddenly had to work together. Since many newly-arrived Saints were from cities, his sermons often included advice about farming or fence building as well as preparing for the last judgment.

What drove Brigham Young? Church enemies saw him as a religious dictator. He acquired plenty of wealth for himself, as did the church, during his thirty-year presidency, and one nickname for him among anti-Mormons was "the Profit."[1] But it was his devotion to Joseph Smith that compelled Brigham to see that Joseph's prophecies came true. If Joseph prophesied that the Rocky Mountains would someday be home to the Saints, then Brigham was determined to make it so. And while Joseph produced the visions of what the church could become, Brigham had the organizational and practical skills to make those visions materialize. Once in Utah, they materialized astoundingly fast.

To be as self-reliant as possible, the church developed many industries to which a particular village might be assigned, such as silk, cotton, sugar, or paper. To the few non-Mormons in the area, the church's growth and business dealings with each other seemed

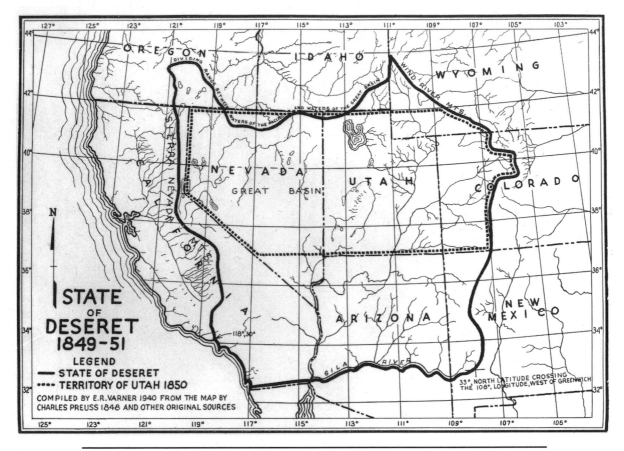

The Mormons envisioned a self-reliant territory that included much of the American west. The territory of Utah recognized by the United States in 1850 consisted of present-day Utah plus most of Nevada and parts of Colorado and Wyoming.

to leave no room for anyone outside the church. Complaints began making their way to Washington, D.C.

The church was always dabbling in new ideas. They considered the English language "God's chosen language" since God had, in their eyes, restored the church of Jesus Christ to an English-speaking man. So the Saints tried to reform the English alphabet by creating thirty-eight new "letters." With these letters, based on sounds, Saints from various nationalities were to be able to communicate more easily. This common "Mormon language" was to parallel the Mormon kingdom, but the plan eventually died.

To non-Mormons, the new language seemed to be some kind of code spelling out treasonous plans. Between the weird new alphabet and the communal way of life the Mormons led that shut out dealings with others, the complaints of non-Mormons increased in volume. In 1857, U.S. President James Buchanan declared the Saints to be in "rebellion." Brigham was notified that he was being replaced as territorial governor and that the federal government itself would assign judges and a governor to the area. During a tenth-anniversary celebration of the founding of Salt Lake City, Brigham learned that an army division was headed for Utah to enforce the new leadership plans.

Some Mormons were incensed that the government was sending troops to the area, and in one case this hostility toward the presence of others turned tragic. Mormon settlers became nervous when a group headed for California, called the Fancher-Baker party, stopped nearby. The Mormons promised the party safe passage if they would lay down their arms. Then a group of Paiute Indians and some Mormon settlers, led by John Doyle Lee, ambushed them. They murdered 120 of them, leaving only 17 young children alive. What became known as the Mountain Meadows Massacre was investigated for years before Lee was arrested, convicted, and executed.

Most Saints, however, did not intend to confront emigrants or government troops. They feared a repeat of their worst days in

Nauvoo or Missouri, so they fled to southern parts of the Salt Lake Valley. The Nauvoo Legion, as the Mormons' militia was still called, remained and prepared to defend the city. A 2,500-man U.S. Army division was wintering in Wyoming, and the Nauvoo Legion set fire to its trains and caused its cattle to stampede. When troops marched through Salt Lake City in June 1858, they saw few citizens except for Mormon men who stood ready with lit torches to burn the city if the army provoked any violence. This time, Brigham told an army captain, the Saints would leave nothing to plunder should anyone try to force them out.

The situation fizzled out when it became obvious to army commanders and the new governor that the Mormons were not government rebels. President Buchanan "pardoned" them, though they had committed no crime that required a pardon. A conflict was avoided, but the U.S. government, as represented by the army, made its presence felt by establishing a camp just south of Salt Lake City.

The Saints' "kingdom" continued to grow, as immigrants from Europe helped fill the Salt Lake Valley. Twenty-two thousand people came to Utah between 1847 and 1856. Most had come from poor cities, but there were many skilled artisans among them, as well as doctors, engineers, and teachers. Farming was the job Young encouraged the most, as it enabled more Saints to be self-sufficient. Families were given only as much farmland as they could work themselves. Everyone helped build homes and roads when a new community was started. Experimental agriculture was exhibited each year at fairs.

Schools were established early in the territory's history. When Salt Lake City was only four years old, most of its wards had school-

Despite many hardships, the Mormons quickly established a thriving community. This drawing shows Salt Lake City in the 1850s.

houses. Young founded Brigham Young Academy in 1875 in Provo, Utah. It became Brigham Young University (BYU) in 1903. Today BYU has an enrollment of more than 10,000 students.

Young built the Salt Lake Theater in the early 1860s to provide additional entertainment for the Saints. He was a regular patron of the theater, and his rocking chair was among its seating for 2,500. The interior was patterned after the Drury Lane Theatre in London, which may have made English Saints feel more at home. Young told a visiting New York critic that he had made the theater's chandelier himself from a gilded cartwheel hung from gilded ox-chains, with vine-like leaves he cut from sheet tin to decorate the candlesticks.

One of Salt Lake City's favorite performers at the theater was humorist Artemus Ward, who worked up a routine that poked fun at polygamy. He called Brigham Young "the most married man I ever saw in my life."[2] Recent immigrants sometimes received the-ater tickets as part of their wages, and box office receipts might have included a bushel of vegetables or a string of sausages as well as cash.

The Salt Lake Tabernacle, with its world-famous acoustics, was completed in 1867, the same year that some Utah settlements became connected by telegraph. With the coming of the railroad, the people of the Salt Lake Valley were no longer so isolated. The cross-country oxcart and handcart days had ended. The area's first temple was dedicated in St. George in 1877, the only temple Brigham would live to see completed.

As Utah Territory became a more vibrant business and cultur-al area, more non-Mormons felt encouraged to move there. The presence of the U.S. military in Utah also encouraged people to move, because it made them feel safer. By 1860, the end of the territory's first decade, its population was about fifty thousand. It already had proved futile to try to defeat the Saints financially, since they were largely self-sufficient, and the army had no reason to attack them.

Those who didn't like the strong influence the Saints had over this growing territory had to try a different way to weaken the Mormons. They went back to 1852, when Brigham Young publicly announced and explained the church's plural marriage doctrine. He had expected that it would not only be tolerated (church leaders believed it to be protected by the U.S. Constitution) but even imitated by other advanced civilizations. A special edition of *The Deseret News* confirmed Brigham's announcement, making official the rumors about plural marriages.

Believing it to be a divine order, the Saints were not ashamed of their plural marriage practice, and so the uproar that followed surprised them. The Mormons even became a tourist attraction. Visitors to Salt Lake City were especially curious about Brigham Young and his numerous wives.

But for many, polygamy was an issue that went beyond curiosity. When the Republican Party was formed in 1854, its platform stated the party's goal to fight polygamy and slavery as "the twin relics of barbarism." Even though the Saints didn't have to build jails in Salt Lake City until a large number of non-Mormons began moving there, they came under attack for their seeming lack of morals in practicing plural marriage.

Actually, only about 10 to 15 percent of Mormon men practiced polygamy, though Americans outside Salt Lake City assumed all Saints were polygamists. Most of the men chose not to practice it, and many couldn't have afforded the expense of supporting more

About 15 percent of Mormon families in the 1800s consisted of a husband, two or more wives, and several children.

than one family. Among the households with plural families, two-thirds of the men had one additional wife.

Many of Brigham Young's wives lived in his spacious Lion House ("Lion" was a nickname for Young), built in a central location of Salt Lake City. Connected to the Lion House was the Beehive House, where Brigham stayed with just one wife at a time, usually a "senior" wife. Still other wives lived in houses in and outside of the city, some in grander homes than others. The Lion House estate also had a schoolhouse for Brigham's fifty-six children, and one of his wives was their teacher. Like other Mormon women, Young's wives made their own and their children's clothing from homespun fabric.

He spent evenings with his wives and children in prayer sessions, after which they all socialized. His older daughters, who later described him as a loving and devoted father, would play the piano and sing. In keeping with Young's belief that the Saints, including Brigham and his wives, needed to enjoy life as well as work hard, social dances were often held in Salt Lake City.

Some plural wives were staunch supporters of "the principle," as it was often called. For many, though, it was difficult to bear. When a new wife entered the household, her presence sometimes caused depression or nervous breakdowns. Wives, who often were sisters, shared housework. Women who had difficulty with polygamy were encouraged by the church to focus on their children or get involved with the church or a career.

Brigham Young's daughter Susa wrote of the happy atmosphere in the main household of the large Young family. One of his wives who divorced him, though, complained in her divorce suit that she had spent more than three years working like a laborer on a farm owned by Young. She went on to say that she seldom saw her husband, and that, despite his multi-million dollar empire, he shared as little of his income with his wives as he could manage.

The non-Mormon public, rather than dissatisfied Mormon wives, were the ones to begin attacking the practice of plural marriage. The first legal attack on plural marriage came in 1862 when Congress passed a law prohibiting polygamy in the United States. It was signed by Republican President Abraham Lincoln. But Lincoln was busy with the Civil War, of course, so he ignored it, as did the Mormons. Most of the juries in court cases were made up of Mormons, and wives seldom testified against their husbands, so polygamy convictions seldom happened.

After the Civil War, Protestant missionaries came to Utah to "save" the Mormon women, or at the least to express sympathy and the disapproval of the outside world. In response, Eliza Snow, a plural widow of Joseph Smith who was then married to Brigham Young (and one of the few prominent women in Latter-day Saint history) led several other Mormon wives in sending a resolution to Congress that defended polygamy.

The government did not recognize plural marriages as legal. Marriage records among the Saints weren't public information, so it was difficult to prove polygamy. Instead, cohabitation (living with a member of the opposite sex outside of marriage) became the "crime" under which Saints were prosecuted. They often received brief jail sentences and fines of a few hundred dollars. Brigham Young himself, finally convicted of "lewd and lascivious cohabitation," was imprisoned in his home in 1870. His personal secretary, George Reynolds, later provided the government with a polygamy "test case," where the guilty verdict was appealed to the

Brigham Young saw the Church of Jesus Christ of Latter-day Saints through dramatic changes. By his death in 1877, the Mormons had finally established a lasting home in Utah.

Supreme Court to test its constitutionality. The final outcome would not be reached until after Young's death.

Generally the Saints led a nonviolent existence in Utah; their struggles now were in the courts and the national media. Some of the judges or governors assigned to Utah by the federal government were more or less impartial in their treatment of the Saints. James McKean, a chief justice of Utah's courts under whose tenureship Brigham Young was home-imprisoned, did all he could to put polygamy on trial. The national media joined the fray when one of Young's wives divorced him and toured the country in the 1870s to lecture to large audiences about the negative side of polygamy.

In August 1877, during his thirtieth year as Church President and Prophet, Brigham Young died. He was seventy-six years old. He had devoted himself to building a society for the Saints, and amid the controversies of his day the Mormons did build a stable and lasting community. His last words were, "Joseph! Joseph! Joseph!" His legacy was the "kingdom" of Utah, with its population of 140,000. Joseph Smith, no doubt, would have been pleased.

FIGHTING FOR RESPECT

7

As with the death of Joseph Smith, it was thought that the Latter-day Saints' church could not continue after Brigham Young died. But church enemies would again be disappointed. The Quorum of Twelve Apostles again led the church, as it had thirty years earlier. It was run by John Taylor, who had almost died in the Illinois jail cell along with Joseph and Hyrum Smith. In 1880 he became the next church president and prophet.

Taylor's presidency was known for its militant stand on the right of the Mormons to practice polygamy at a time when the United States government was most determined to stamp it out. Taylor was an English immigrant who was converted in Canada in 1836 and helped shape the successful missionary work in England. He'd seen Joseph and Hyrum die for the rights of the Saints to practice their religion and was not about to give up any of it.

In 1879, two years after Young's death, the Supreme Court upheld the guilty verdict in the George Reynolds polygamy case.

Reynolds, Young's secretary, had been convicted of polygamy in 1874. Once the highest court in the land had ruled it permissible for the government to prosecute the Saints for polygamy, the fight got intense.

Taylor, who had seven wives and thirty-four children, defended plural marriage, stating: "We acknowledge our children; we acknowledge our wives. We have no mistresses."[1] Newspapers all over the country, including the anti-Mormon Salt Lake City *Tribune,* criticized the Saints. The *Tribune* quoted Taylor as declaring: "God is greater than the United States. . . . I defy the United States. I will obey God."[2]

By 1881, just after the church celebrated its fiftieth anniversary, Utah had a mostly-Mormon population of nearly 144,000, some 60,000 of whom had arrived in the past decade. With the bad publicity from plural marriage, life became difficult for Saints outside Utah, especially in southern states. Some were beaten by mobs and a few were murdered.

In 1882, Congress passed a law making it illegal for any polygamist to vote or hold public office. Voters were required to swear, under oath, that they were not part of a polygamous marriage. This law left Utah's Mormon residents under state and local governments led by non-Mormons. Mormon men in leadership positions, who tended to practice polygamy, went "underground." They lived in Latter-day Saint settlements in Canada or Mexico, or kept their Rocky Mountain whereabouts unknown to avoid arrest. Houses were equipped with trapdoors to hide polygamous husbands quickly, if need be. Women were imprisoned for refusing to testify against their husbands, and hundreds of men were jailed for "unlawful cohabitation." Even children were questioned by federal agents to get information on their parents.

In 1887, the federal government fired its big guns in the war against polygamy: the Edmunds-Tucker Act, passed by Congress, declared adultery to be a felony. Performing a marriage that was not made public record also became a felony (polygamous marriages were performed in secret). The government also now had the right to assume ownership of all church property worth more than $50,000. On the door of the Salt Lake Tabernacle, for example, hung the sign: FOR RENT. SEE U.S. MARSHALL. The Saints had to rent their own property. The Perpetual Emigrating Fund Company was abolished and all its funds confiscated by the federal government. All Mormon schools were closed.

From his "underground" hiding place in Davis County, Utah, church president Taylor sent word to the Saints that the government persecution of polygamy was "medieval." He urged Saints to remain faithful to their religion despite the current hardships of doing so.

Taylor died the year the Edmunds-Tucker Act was passed. He had served as church president seven years. With his death, the Saints, again under the temporary leadership of the Apostles, turned to the idea of giving up "the principle." Mormon lobbyists in Washington, D.C., found that statehood, something the church greatly desired for Utah, would never be granted if polygamy continued. The Supreme Court upheld the Edmunds-Tucker Act, declaring the Latter-day Saints to be in "open rebellion" against the U.S. government. The Court claimed the church was keeping its members under "absolute ecclesiastical control." The Mountain Meadows Massacre of 1857 had many Americans thinking that the Mormons bloodily avenged their grievances.

Almost every prominent leader among the Saints was either in

The controversy over plural marriages attracted much negative publicity for the church. Some political cartoons, such as this representation of the Edmunds-Tucker Act of 1887, suggested that the United States used polygamy as a way of shutting down the church; but some people's real fear was the Mormons' continuing economic and political power.

jail, had served time in prison, or was hiding out on the underground. Even plural wives began living life on the run. Congress was considering a bill that would deny U.S. citizenship for the Saints.

Wilford Woodruff, from whose wagon Brigham Young had first gazed upon the Salt Lake Valley, became at age eighty-two the fourth Church President and Prophet in 1889. It was under his leadership that the Saints began to compromise "the principle."

A judge from New York, Elliot Sandford, who was sympathetic to the plight of the Mormons, was appointed chief justice of Utah. Once Sandford arrived, church first counselor and polygamist George Q. Cannon gave himself up, receiving a lenient sentence of a $450 fine and seventy-five days in jail. Hundreds of Mormon men followed that example, and church president Woodruff, as a goodwill gesture, had the Endowment House, where many of the secret plural marriage ceremonies were performed, torn down. In an address to Congress, U.S. President Grover Cleveland declared polygamy to be nearly abolished.

But when Benjamin Harrison became U.S. president in March 1889, his attorney general requested the resignation of Elliot Sandford. Sandford was replaced by Charles Zane, a judge who had already shown his dislike for polygamists during a previous tenure in Utah. Then, one of the courts in Utah denied citizenship rights to recently emigrated Saints. This was a blow to the voting power of the church. Just as it began to seem they were clearing, the dark clouds hanging over the Saints in Utah were gathering again.

In December 1889, church president Woodruff and the twelve Apostles signed a statement announcing that the Saints were entering a new era. They claimed their values had changed, that the church did not control almost every aspect of life in Utah or seek bloody revenge on its enemies. It was difficult to deny that church leaders played a large part in Utah's economy and government, and that all church decisions made at its higher levels would be automatically approved by the general membership. But the statement by Woodruff and the Apostles signaled to the Saints that a new era *was* beginning for them. It was the elderly Woodruff's job to lead the Saints in a new direction.

Voters in Idaho were required to take an oath that they did not belong to any organization or association that advocated polygamy, and that oath was upheld by the Supreme Court. This led Woodruff in 1890 to issue another statement, or "manifesto," that discouraged Saints from entering into any new plural marriages. The Quorum of Twelve wept as they approved the manifesto, while Woodruff assured them that God would not let him lead the Saints astray.

The pressure applied by the U.S. government, and the desire for statehood and a place in mainstream America, had finally won over the Saints' strong streak of independence. Polygamy still would be practiced "underground" for several more years, and some non-Mormons would make a hobby of proving it. But the church had turned a corner, on the way to becoming a part of twentieth-century America.

In 1891, the church suggested that the political parties of Utah—the People's Party, with its Mormon members, and the Liberal Party, joined by non-Mormons—begin to associate with the country's two main political parties, the Republicans and the Democrats. It wasn't so unusual now to have Saints run against each other for office.

Amid their political problems, in 1893 the Saints were able to celebrate the dedication of the Salt Lake Temple, forty years after its

The completion of the spectacular Mormon Temple in 1893 represented the church's stability and the Mormons' efforts to enter the modern era.

cornerstones were laid, forty-six years after its site was dedicated by Brigham Young, and on the sixty-third anniversary of the church's founding. The temple's walls are 6 feet (1.8 m) thick, made from granite hauled by teams of oxen from Little Cottonwood Canyon, 20 miles (32 km) away. As a symbol of the new era the Saints were entering, the temple was completed when its capstone was put in place with the press of an electric button.

The dedication service included a ten-page prayer of blessing read by Wilford Woodruff. He asked God to bless every aspect of the building, including "the connecting pipes and wires," "the mortar and plaster," as well as "seats, cushions [and] curtains."[3] Trains brought Saints to Salt Lake City from all over the territory, and the dedication service was repeated twice daily for at least seventy-five thousand Saints over a seventeen-day period.

By the next year, President Harrison offered "full amnesty and pardon" to polygamists who had entered into plural marriage before Woodruff's Manifesto of 1890. All Utah residents, including Mormons, could now run for and hold political office in the territory.[4]

The Salt Lake Tabernacle Choir, which traced its beginnings to the church's pioneer days of crossing the plains, visited Illinois, the state that expelled the Saints less than fifty years earlier. The choir took second place in a competition at the World's Columbian Exposition, or World's Fair, in Chicago, showing America a positive side of the church.

On January 4, 1896, *The Deseret News* announced the long-awaited prize the church had sought for decades: on its seventh try, Utah had been granted statehood. Bells rang, whistles tooted, and crowds filled the streets to celebrate. The Church of Jesus Christ of Latter-day Saints, which began in the United States, then left it, was a part of it again.

In Salt Lake City, residents crowded the streets to celebrate Utah's statehood on January 4, 1896.

THE CHURCH SPREADS 'ROUND THE WORLD

8

The Church of Jesus Christ of Latter-day Saints had passed a milestone in its relationship with the United States of America. Now it looked inward to address problems that had accumulated while it worked to become a part of America.

Buying land in Utah, sending missionaries abroad and around the United States, and building schools, meeting halls, and temples had left the church with a large debt. And, though they had finally won statehood for Utah by appearing to give up polygamy, plural marriage would continue to be a problem for the Saints for at least another decade.

Wilford Woodruff advised the Saints during his presidency not to wait so long to appoint new church presidents, so when he died in 1898, his successor, Lorenzo Snow, became President within eleven days. Snow had been jailed three times for polygamy, but his biggest concern as church president was debt.

Snow realized that if more (many more!) church members

began tithing (giving 10 percent of their income to the church), that debt could disappear. He began to make it the theme of his appearances; at one of the twice-yearly church conferences held for all members, he told his fellow Saints that tithing would bring them spiritual blessings and divine protection. Tithing, in fact, might have prevented all the abuse the Saints had suffered in the past, Snow preached. Saints became more generous, and money became less of a problem for the church.

Plural marriage made a comeback in newspaper headlines, though, when Utah elected a polygamist, Brigham H. Roberts, to Congress in 1898. Christian ministers sent word from Utah that a polygamist was headed for Washington, D.C., and petitions against Roberts, signed by millions of people, were sent to Congress. Lorenzo Snow tried to convince Americans, in a letter to New York newspapers, that the church did not teach polygamy anymore, but Congress voted overwhelmingly not to let Roberts serve.

When Lorenzo Snow died in 1901, church finances were in much better shape. They also became the subject of the next national investigation into church affairs. Snow's successor was Joseph Fielding Smith, the son of Hyrum Smith. After Hyrum's death, young Joseph F. Smith (whose mother became a plural wife of Heber Kimball) had come to Utah with the other Mormon wagon trains, driving an ox team himself at the age of nine.

During Joseph F. Smith's church presidency, a Latter-day Saint named Reed Smoot was elected to the Senate. Smoot did not practice polygamy, so other U.S. senators looked closely at church finances in trying to decide whether a Mormon should be allowed to hold office.

In addition to the conclusion by non-Mormons that all Saints practiced polygamy, it was also thought that the Mormon church was as much a business empire as a religion, with members tithing their income and making church leaders rich. After all, Joseph Smith and Brigham Young had dabbled in banking and real estate businesses while running the church. Young had died a millionaire.

Joseph F. Smith, testifying about church finances before the Senate, admitted that as head of the Church of Jesus Christ of Latter-day Saints, he also was president of the largest retail operation in Utah, two banks, the Utah Sugar Company, a railroad, and more. He also admitted to practicing polygamy since the 1890 Manifesto (those already in plural marriages by 1890 weren't supposed to desert their families). Nevertheless, the Senate voted to allow Smoot to hold the seat to which he was elected. He went on to serve as a Utah senator for thirty years.

In the meantime, church president Smith had to reissue a statement against polygamy. It wouldn't be the last, as the anti-Mormon Salt Lake City *Tribune* continued to publish names of prominent church members still practicing it. Overall, in the state of Utah, Saints and "gentiles" (as the Saints referred to non-Mormons) continued to squabble over church wealth, polygamy, and politics. The negative publicity spread to England, where Saints were subjected to anti-Mormon violence, and Germany, where some church leaders were forced to leave the country.

Joseph F. Smith, son of Hyrum Smith and fourth president of the Latter-day Saints, defended the Mormons' economic growth before a U.S. Senate committee.

Once again, the Tabernacle Choir provided the church some good publicity. Accepting an invitation to sing in New York City in 1911, the choir then toured more than two dozen cities and even sang before President William Taft. Their success enabled Saints and "gentiles" to interact in a positive way. With the outbreak of World War I in Europe a few years later, almost fifteen thousand church members served with the U.S. armed forces. This also improved the general public's perception of the Latter-day Saints.

Joseph F. Smith had established a Bureau of Information within the church for visitors to Salt Lake City, and the barriers between Latter-day Saints and mainstream America gradually shrank. When Joseph F. Smith died in 1918, the normally anti-Mormon Salt Lake City *Tribune* gave him a polite obituary. Also, Utah's voters, 75 percent of whom were Mormons, elected a Jewish man, Simon Bamberger, as governor.

When the church celebrated its centennial (hundred-year anniversary) in April 1930, Saints who weren't able to attend services in Salt Lake City could hear them broadcast over the radio. A church pageant, "Message of the Ages," ran for a month. Though the employment difficulties of the Great Depression were starting to be felt by those in Utah as well as all over America, church president Heber Grant lifted the Saints' spirits during the anniversary services by stressing achievements made by Latter-day Saints in the church's first century. He even let Saints take some credit for advances in science and technology, telling them it wasn't just a coincidence that those advances began to occur at the same time as Joseph Smith's visions.

Grant also revived one of Smith's visions that was originally just advice: The Word of Wisdom, which came to Joseph in Kirtland, Ohio, in 1833. The Word of Wisdom warned Saints to avoid tobacco, "strong" drink, or alcohol, and "hot" drinks (coffee and tea), and to eat meat sparingly. It hadn't been a strict rule, though. Coffee and tea, in fact, were part of the pioneer Saints' food rations, and vineyards for homemade wine were common in Utah. Under Grant, it became an important part of church doctrine, and those Saints who didn't follow it would not be admitted to the temple.

The "typical" Mormon community slowly began to change as missionaries started forming communities in southern states such as Florida and Georgia. Many other Saints began moving from the Rocky Mountains to California in search of more economic opportunities. Though it was thought at first that true Latter-day Saint leaders must come from the Rocky Mountains and be descendants of Mormon pioneers, by the 1940s Latter-day Saint communities outside of the Wasatch Range could be led by local converts.

When Heber Grant died in 1945, his twenty-seven-year presidency saw the church grow from 83 stakes, or districts, to 149 stakes in the United States, and there were almost one million members. The church also now owned several sites of historical importance, such as the Vermont farmhouse where Joseph Smith was born and the Sacred Grove in New York, where Smith had his first vision.

During David McKay's church presidency in the 1950s and 1960s, Latter-day Saint missionary efforts doubled. Construction of temples began in Europe, and converts were no longer asked to come to the United States. "Zion," McKay said, is wherever the "pure in heart" live. For the first time, stakes were formed outside the U.S. Mexico, for example, now has 700,000 members. In 1970, when McKay died at age ninety-six, the church had grown to three million members.

McKay tried to increase awareness of and interest in the church in the 1960s with his "Every Member a Missionary" program. Saints were encouraged to get involved in their communities outside of the church, and promote their faith by their lifestyle examples. Church members were told to ask the "Golden Questions" of friends, neighbors, and other acquaintances: "What do you know about the Mormons? Would you like to know more?"

Another church program, called "family home evening," was developed in the 1960s to help the children in Mormon families. This was one night each week when family members put aside other commitments to be together, and parents and children could discuss church teachings and doctrine. Family home evenings came about when American youths in general were rebelling against their parents' culture. Today, the once-a-week family time remains a key part of how Mormon parents pass their faith on to their children.

A major change in church policy came in the late 1970s, when church president Spencer Kimball (Heber Kimball's grandson) opened the church priesthood to male members of African descent. This had been denied them since Joseph Smith's days, when he claimed to receive the information from God that Africans were descended from Cain, who is described in the Bible as the first murderer. Spencer Kimball and the church's twelve apostles put the matter to a special prayer session. Soon black members were ordained and given levels of church leadership equal to that of other Saints around the world.

Today the Church of Jesus Christ of Latter-day Saints claims at least 9 million members in more than 150 countries and territories. About 4.5 million live in the United States, making it the sixth-largest religious denomination in the country. The church's annual income, estimated to be approximately $4.7 billion, continues to be an issue raised by church outsiders. Church income supports Mormon schools such as Brigham Young University, missions, and temple building, with leftover money being reinvested. Church leaders, such as ward bishops, are not paid and serve voluntarily. The church's current president is Gordon B. Hinckley, who, like all previous leaders of the church, is seen by Saints as a living prophet who communicates directly with God.

The typical Latter-day Saint missionary today is a young, single church member, most likely male, whose missionary life is supported by his or her parents. In recent years, many retired couples have also signed up for missionary tours. A Latter-day Saint missionary works long days, six days a week, for two years (or eighteen months for young women), calling on people at their homes, distributing *The Book of Mormon* to those who are interested, and hoping to win at least a few converts per year. In recent years, Latin America, which now has 2.7 million church members, has been one of the church's biggest success stories. Africa has also become a fast-growing region for the church.

Some Latter-day Saints have complained that excommunication awaits any who challenge church doctrine. In the last few years, for example, church members claimed they were excommunicated for expressing the belief that Joseph Smith wrote *The Book of Mormon* without divine inspiration, or for doing research showing the church secretly allowed polygamy to continue after the 1890 Manifesto.

Some women members of the church have been "disfellowshipped," or banned from receiving church sacraments, for their practice of praying to the heavenly wife of God. Mormons believe that she exists but feel that prayers should not be addressed to Her.

The scriptural basis for their objection to these prayers is that the Lord's Prayer addresses God the Father, so Jesus did not intend prayers for Her based on the Scripture. The Relief Society for women, which began in Nauvoo, now must answer to ward bishops. Women do preach during church services, however, and can lead some church organizations.

The Latter-day Saint church and the surviving group that splintered off from it, the Reorganized Church of Jesus Christ of Latter Day Saints (RLDS), have been on better terms in recent years. The RLDS church, founded in Independence, Missouri, now has a membership of more than 200,000. They run their church similarly to the Mormon church, with a church presidency and a Quorum of Twelve Apostles. The descendants of Hyrum Smith (from the LDS church) and of Joseph Smith (from the RLDS church) gather regularly now for family reunions.

What does life within the Church of Jesus Christ of Latter-day Saints hold for its faithful members? How does it influence their daily lives? Lloyd and Judy Abbott, of Frederick, Maryland, and their family of nine children, two sons-in-law, and one grandchild provide many examples of that influence.

On one family home evening, with nine family members gathered after dinner, daughter Kristen and her husband, Nathan

---

Gordon Hinckley presides over a church that has expanded far beyond Utah during the twentieth century. This photograph shows Mr. Hinckley and his wife in front of a Mormon temple in Mexico. About one-fourth of the church's nine million members live in Latin America.

Most Latter-day Saints missionaries are either young men or retired couples. These American missionaries traveled to Australia, where church membership has grown to more than 60,000.

Kleinman, had prepared a discussion based on a passage from *The Book of Mormon.* "We are connected to our ancestors," Kristen told the group, "as well as our descendants, and we can show our respect for all of them by the kind of life we lead. We are not just 'floating' individuals, but linked to and responsible to family members who came before and who will come after us."

Son Aaron had returned a couple of months earlier from his missionary tour of Germany, where he and a partner (missionaries always travel in pairs) put in fifteen-hour days, six days a week, for two years. "We were supposed to be up at six and study Scripture." Then, after breakfast, they studied the German language before going out to large apartment complexes to ring doorbells and attempt to distribute *The Book of Mormon,* returning home to their modest apartment by 9:30 P.M.

In Germany, Aaron said, converts were not easily won. "A missionary is lucky to baptize two or three" new church members. Now Aaron is working to save money to attend church-run Brigham Young University in Utah, where his sisters Jennifer and Emily are students. The university charges less tuition for tithing church members, who might spend thousands of dollars to support a son or daughter working as a missionary.

For the Abbotts' two children in high school, Mary Ruth and Joshua, religion classes are a part of their normal school day, though they go to public schools. The Latter-day Saints' local meeting place, where the Abbotts spend three hours each Sunday afternoon, also has weekday religion classes for its high school-age members. Mary Ruth and Joshua spend forty-five minutes each morning learning about Scripture (from the Bible and from *The Book of Mormon*) and church history before being carpooled to their public schools.

At age fifteen, Joshua is following in his father Lloyd's and older brother Aaron's footsteps to Latter-day Saint manhood: boys can become church deacons at age twelve, before becoming teachers, then priests, and finally elders. Once an elder, a young man is eligible for missionary work and can baptize his converts. As a teacher, Joshua helps prepare the Sacrament (similar to what other churches call communion, or the sharing of bread and wine, which the Bible says Jesus of Nazareth did at his Last Supper with his twelve apostles) each Sunday for worship services.

He also shares a regular responsibility with his father: "I have to go out with my dad once a month for home-teaching families." Each family in the church has a "home-teacher," that is, another church member who visits them monthly to make sure the family is doing well. In March 1993, a violent snowstorm hit the eastern United States, and "the first thing everybody did, during the blizzard, was call their home-teaching families to see if they were OK," said Judy.

On Sundays, everyone attends church for three hours. Each attends the Sacrament Meeting, or church service, for one hour. It features preaching by men and women (all adult church members take turns speaking), singing, praying, and distribution of the Sacrament. Everyone, from the youngest to the oldest, has a Sunday School class for an hour, and then the third hour is spent with men and women, boys and girls meeting for different organizations: Ruth and thirteen-year-old Mary Ellen will attend meetings of the Young Women's organization, Judy and Kristen will go to a Relief Society meeting, and Lloyd and his two older sons attend priesthood meetings. Ben and Joshua are in the Boy Scouts, which their church helps sponsor.

The Abbotts' church ward has a bus that makes the fifty-minute trip each month for any member who wants to go to the nearest temple, in Washington, D.C. The temple does not admit non-Mormons or Saints who haven't been issued a yearly temple pass from their bishops. It is here that many of the church's special ordinances take place, such as baptism for the dead or the endowment, as well as family "sealings," which the church says keeps families united throughout eternity. In addition to baptisms, church members can have sealings performed for their ancestors' families, if they have their names, as well as their own. Weddings also are held at the temples.

In addition to tithing, Latter-day Saint church members like the Abbotts are asked to fast one Sunday each month, and the money saved by not eating is donated to charity. Also, each ward has a missionary fund that everyone is asked to help with, for families who can't meet all the expenses of paying for their children's missionary trips.

Family vacations might mean taking in the pageants, or dramas, that the church presents in historic areas such as Nauvoo, Illinois; Palmyra, New York (where Joseph Smith had his first vision); or in the Rocky Mountains. The pageant at Hill Cumorah, Judy said, is spectacular.

A few years ago, Lloyd Abbott lost the job that supported his family. While he and Judy looked for work, the family was supported by the church. The church encourages its members to turn to it for financial help when they need it, rather than the government.

In short, one could say that the Church of Jesus Christ of Latter-day Saints expects many things of its members: tithing, following the Word of Wisdom, time spent as missionaries, and a life that includes many hours devoted to church service. On the other hand, the church offers its members, who call each other "Brother" and "Sister" (as in Brother Lloyd, or Sister Judy), emotional and financial support when it's needed, from making sure everyone is aware of needs of their "home-teaching" families, to subsidized tuition at Brigham Young University. "It's about standards," said Kristen Abbott Kleinman. "High standards."

SOURCE NOTES

Chapter Two

1. Smith, Joseph. *The Pearl of Great Price* (Salt Lake City: Church of Jesus Christ of Latter-day Saints, 1982), p. 48.
2. Ibid., p. 49.
3. Ibid., p. 50.
4. Ibid., p. 51.
5. Ibid., p. 55.
6. Smith, Joseph F., *Essentials in Church History* (Salt Lake City: Deseret Book Co., 1972), p. 74.
7. Ibid., p. 84.
8. Newall, Linda King, and Valeen Tippetts Avery, *Mormon Enigma: Emma Hale Smith* (Champaign, Ill.: University of Illinois Press, 1984), p. 57.
9. Ibid., p. 72.
10. Smith, *Essentials in Church History*, p. 191.

Chapter Three

1. Smith, Joseph F., *Essentials in Church History* (Salt Lake City: Deseret Book Co., 1972), pp. 250–251.
2. Smith, *Essentials in Church History*, p. 307.
3. Ibid., p. 309.

Chapter Four

1. Newall, Linda King, and Valeen Tippetts Avery, *Mormon Enigma: Emma Hale Smith* (Champaign, Ill.: University of Illinois Press, 1984), p. 194.
2. Ibid., p. 172.
3. Smith, Joseph F., *Essentials in Church History* (Salt Lake City: Deseret Book Co., 1972), p. 370.

Chapter Five

1. *American Heritage* (April 1993), pp. 74–76.
2. "Come, Come Ye Saints," from *Hymns of the Church of Jesus Christ of Latter-day Saints.*

Chapter Six

1. *American Heritage* (April 1993), pp. 72.
2. Wallace, Irving, *Twenty-Seventh Wife* (New York: Simon & Schuster, 1961), p. 142.

Chapter Seven

1. Smith, Joseph F., *Essentials in Church History* (Salt Lake City: Deseret Book Co., 1972), p. 470.
2. Taylor, Samuel W., *Rocky Mountain Empire: The Latter-day Saints Today* (New York: Macmillan Publishing Co., 1978), p. 29.
3. Ibid., p. 50.
4. Ibid.

FOR FURTHER READING

Bernotas, Bob. *Brigham Young*. New York: Chelsea House, 1993.

Burton, Sir Richard F. *The City of the Saints, and across the Rocky Mountains to California*. New York: Knopf, 1963.

Doubleday, Veronica. *Salt Lake City*. New York: Macmillan Children's Group, 1994.

Edwards, Paul M. *Our Legacy of Faith: A Brief History of the Reorganized Church of Jesus Christ of Latter Day Saints*. Independence, Mo.: Herald House, 1991.

Elgin, Kathleen. *The Mormons: The Church of Jesus Christ of Latter-day Saints*. New York: McKay, 1969.

Gates, Susa Young. *The Life Story of Brigham Young*. New York: Macmillan, 1930.

Hughes, Dean, and Tom Hughes. *Great Stories from Mormon History*. Salt Lake City, Utah: Deseret Books, 1994.

McCloud, Susan E. *Joseph Smith: A Photobiography*. Murray, Utah: Aspen Books, 1992.

Madsen, Susan A. *I Walked to Zion: True Stories of Youth Who Walked the Mormon Trail.* Salt Lake City, Utah: Deseret Books, 1994.

Taylor, Samuel W. *Family Kingdom.* New York: McGraw-Hill, 1951.

Thompson, Roger. *The Mormon Church.* New York: Hippocrene Books, 1993.

West, Ray B. *The Kingdom of the Saints; the Story of Brigham Young and the Mormons.* New York: Viking Press, 1957.

INTERNET SITES

Due to the changeable nature of the Internet, sites appear and disappear very quickly. Following are examples of the myriad of resources that provide useful information on the Church of Jesus Christ of Latter-day Saints. Internet addresses must be entered with capital and lowercase letters exactly as they appear.

LDS connect is an interactive information service for Latter-day Saints:

http://miracomm.com/

Evidences for the *Book of Mormon* is a Web site dedicated to providing evidence that the *Book of Mormon* is an authentic ancient text:

http://www.athenet.net/~jlindsay/BMEvidences.shtml

Church*talk* is an information page for Saints and others who want to know more about the Church of Jesus Christ of Latter-day Saints:

http://www.teleport.com/~love

INDEX

ABOUT THE AUTHOR

Jean Kinney Williams grew up in Ohio and lives there now with her husband and four children. She studied journalism in college and, in addition to writing, enjoys reading, volunteering at church, and spending time with her family. She is the author of the Franklin Watts First Book *Matthew Hensen: Polar Adventurer* (1994) and of another American Religious Experience book, *The Amish* (1996).